FRIENDS

Tell the TRUTH

by **Megan Borgert-Spaniol**

PEBBLE
a capstone imprint

Published by Pebble, an imprint of Capstone.
1710 Roe Crest Drive
North Mankato, Minnesota 56003
capstonepub.com

**Library of Congress Cataloging-in-Publication Data is available on
the Library of Congress website.**
ISBN: 9781666315608 (hardcover)
ISBN: 9781666320145 (paperback)
ISBN: 9781666315660 (ebook PDF)

Summary: Being honest isn't always easy. Sometimes the truth is
embarrassing or upsetting. But a good friend tells the truth. This
means admitting mistakes, sharing how you truly feel, and more.
Learn how to be a good friend by telling the truth!

Editorial and Design Credits
Editor: Jessica Rusick, Mighty Media; Designer: Aruna Rangarajan,
Mighty Media

Image Credits
Shutterstock: Andrew Angelov, 21, A3pfamily, 19, Golden Pixels
LLC, 5, gpointstudio, 13, Pressmaster, 7, Robert Kneschke, Cover,
Sudowoodo, 20, Veja, 10, 11, wavebreakmedia, 9, 15, 17

Design Elements: Mighty Media, Inc.

All internet sites appearing in back matter were available and
accurate when this book was sent to press.

TABLE OF CONTENTS

Words in **bold** are in the glossary.

Lost Chalk

Your friend comes over to your house. She brings her sidewalk chalk. She takes the chalk when she leaves. But later, you notice she left some pieces behind.

Your friend calls you. She asks if you've seen her chalk. You decide to tell the truth. This means being **honest** about what happened.

Admit Mistakes

You can tell the truth by **admitting** to **mistakes**. You **accidentally** spill paint on your friend's shirt. She doesn't notice.

You feel bad. You want to pretend it didn't happen. But you decide to tell your friend. You say you are sorry. She is **upset**. But she is also glad you were honest.

Reasons Why

You can also be honest about why something happened. Your friend asks you to meet her after school. But you forget.

The next day, your friend asks where you were. You think about making up a reason. Instead, you tell her you forgot. Then you say you're sorry.

Feelings

You can also tell the truth about your feelings. Your friend didn't come over to play after school. This made you feel sad.

The next day, your friend asks what's wrong. You almost say nothing is wrong. But this isn't true. You tell him why you feel upset. This helps you both feel better!

No Rumors

Your classmate leaves school early. Your friend wonders if he got in trouble. She says this to others. Soon, everyone thinks your classmate got in trouble.

Your friend created a **rumor**. This is a story that may not be true. Nobody knows why your classmate left. It is not nice to make up things about people.

Hard Truth

Telling the truth isn't always easy.
Your friend is trying out for a talent show.
He wants to play a song on his guitar.
He says he just learned it.

He plays the song for you. Then he asks
if you like it. You think your friend needs
more practice. You don't think he knows
the new song yet.

You don't want to hurt your friend's feelings. But you want him to get in the show.

You decide to tell the truth kindly. You suggest he play another song. You ask if there is one he knows better. Your friend listens to you. He gets in the talent show!

Gaining Trust

Telling the truth helps you gain **trust**. Your friend tells you she is moving. She asks you not to tell others. You don't tell anyone. But other people find out.

You tell your friend you didn't say anything. She knows that you tell the truth. So, she trusts you. She believes you are being honest.

Practice Telling the Truth

It's important to tell friends the truth. Practice telling the truth by doing a trust walk with a friend!

WHAT YOU DO:

1. Find a safe, open space. Place toys or other objects in the space.

2. Decide who will go first. Put a blindfold over that person's eyes.

3. Have the blindfolded person walk slowly across the space. The other person tells the blindfolded person where to walk to avoid the objects.

4. Switch places. The person who was the guide will now be blindfolded.

Glossary

accidentally (AK-suh-duhnt-uhl-ee)—without meaning to

admit (ad-MIT)—to say you did something wrong

honest (AHN-ust)—to be truthful. People who are honest do not lie.

mistake (muh-STAKE)—something done wrong without meaning to

rumor (ROO-mur)—something said by many people although it may not be true

trust (TRUHST)—to believe that people will be honest and do what they say they're going to do. If you trust someone, you believe them and believe IN them.

upset (uhp-SEHT)—unhappy or angry

Read More

Honders, Christine. *Why Is Cheating Wrong?* New York: PowerKids Press, 2019.

Newman, Jeff. *Found.* New York: Simon & Schuster Books for Young Readers, 2018.

Santos, Rita. *Zoom in on Honesty.* New York: Enslow Publishing, 2018.

Internet Sites

KidsHealth—Cheating
kidshealth.org/en/kids/cheating.html#catschool

KidsHealth—Gossip
kidshealth.org/en/kids/gossip.html#catfriend

PBSKids: Arthur—Francine's Tough Day
pbskids.org/arthur/friends/francines-tough-day

Index

About the Author

Megan Borgert-Spaniol is an author and editor of children's media. When she isn't writing or reading, she enjoys doing yoga, eating croissants, and crafting homemade pizzas. Megan lives in Minneapolis, Minnesota, with a tall, goofy man and a small, chatty cat.